essential careers™

A CAREER AS AN
ELECTRICIAN

DANIEL E. HARMON

ROSEN
PUBLISHING®

NEW YORK

Published in 2011 by The Rosen Publishing Group, Inc.
29 East 21st Street, New York, NY 10010

Library of Congress Cataloging-in-Publication Data

Harmon, Daniel E.
A career as an electrician / Daniel E. Harmon.—1st ed.
   p. cm.—(Essential careers)
Includes bibliographical references and index.
ISBN 978-1-4358-9470-9 (library binding)
1. Electrical engineering—Vocational guidance—Juvenile literature.
2. Electricians—Juvenile literature. I. Title.
TK159.H37 2011
621.319'24023—dc22

                              2009044041

Manufactured in the United States of America

CPSIA Compliance Information: Batch #S10YA: For further information, contact Rosen Publishing, New York, New York, at 1-800-237-9932.

contents

INTRO

Inside a breaker box is a baffling arrangement of color-coded wires and switches. A skilled electrician often can spot a problem at a glance.

DUCTION

Americans rely on electricity. It provides much more than light, heat, and air-conditioning. It also runs countless appliances, from televisions to toasters, clocks to computers.

Any general book on home and building maintenance reveals how vital electricity is to the entire structure. Except for the basic parts of the structure—the foundation, frame, windows, doors, and plumbing—electricity is involved. (In many buildings, it interacts with those basic parts, too.) It blows hot and cold air through heating and air-conditioning systems. It makes hot water. Electric ceiling fans help circulate air. Electricity powers appliances large and small: refrigerators and freezers, ranges and ovens, microwave ovens, dishwashers, clothes washers and dryers, icemakers, garbage disposals, vacuum cleaners, and many more.

Think about what happens when something goes wrong with the electrical current. Homes that are heated and air-conditioned with electric units quickly become dreadfully cold in the winter and hot in the summer. After a few hours, whatever is in the refrigerator begins to go bad. There can be no cooking in stoves, toasters, or conventional and microwave ovens. Clothes cannot be washed or dried. The only hot water available is what is currently in the hot water tank (which is beginning to cool). As for hair dryers and curlers, televisions, desktop computers, power treadmills, and other conveniences—forget those.

Keeping society "powered" is the extremely important job of electricians. Even under normal circumstances, consumers

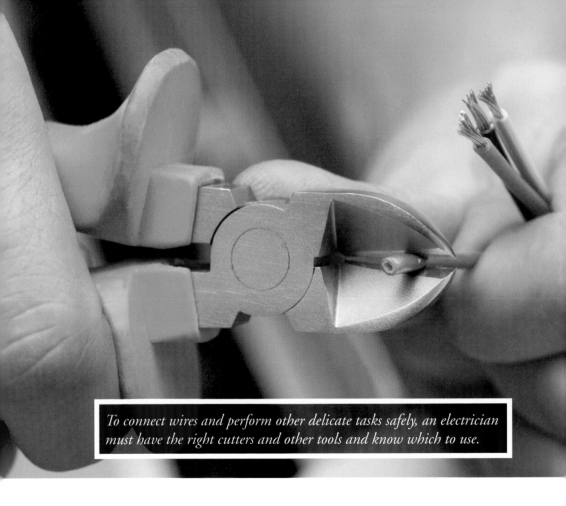

To connect wires and perform other delicate tasks safely, an electrician must have the right cutters and other tools and know which to use.

have to be sure their electrical systems and appliances are in good order. Home wiring must be inspected for hazards from time to time. Repairs must be made on many different items. Wiring and electrical units must be replaced occasionally.

Electricians are hired to perform two kinds of work: new and old. In a slow economy, they receive little new work. People and companies cannot afford to build new homes and factories, which call for electrical installations. However, society always needs to keep existing electrical lines and products in efficient, safe working condition. That's what makes the electrician's career essential and recession-proof.

Many young people are interested in becoming electricians. It's a wise career choice. Regardless of the state of the economy, electricians will always be in demand. Laurence Shatkin, a noted occupational expert, includes electricians in his 2009 book, *Great Jobs in the President's Stimulus Plan*. He cites this career path among the "jobs that are more likely to offer hiring opportunities as the recovery package takes effect." Shatkin also includes electrical and electronics repairers in another book, *150 Best Recession-Proof Jobs*.

People can do without new clothes, but they can't do without good lighting and heating. They can do without a nice long vacation in July, but they can't do without a new furnace if the old one fails in January. They can work without electrical tools in the yard, but they're lost without their computers. Even after new sources of raw power—solar, wind, and water—eventually become common, electricity will continue to be society's power connector.

People use electricity for hundreds of purposes in everyday life and work. Because of that, they need professional workers who can keep the power on and keep their products working properly.

chapter 1

WHAT DOES AN ELECTRICIAN DO?

The *Occupational Outlook Handbook*, published by the U.S. Department of Labor's Bureau of Labor Statistics (BLS), describes the basic job role of electricians this way: "Electricians bring electricity into homes, businesses, and factories. They install and maintain the wiring, fuses, and other components through which electricity flows. Many electricians also install electrical machines in factories."

There are many kinds of electricians. Some work inside homes. Some work inside large facilities, such as hospitals and college buildings. Some work in factories. Some work on the electrical parts of heavy equipment or computer systems, not on buildings.

The National Joint Apprenticeship and Training Committee categorizes most electricians' roles into the following four general areas:

Outside lineman. This worker installs and maintains transmission and distribution lines from power plants to homes, businesses, and factories.

Inside wireman. This type of electrician installs the power and lighting systems in new office buildings and industrial facilities. The inside wireman also services electrical systems in existing structures.

Linemen frequently work at formidable heights to make repairs, replace-
ments, and adjustments. Here, a lineman is perched on a pylon tower.

Residential wireman. Like the inside wireman, this professional installs new electrical systems and maintains old ones but works primarily in homes and housing complexes.

VDV installer technician. Telephone and computer systems are the specialty areas of this type of electrician. Phone circuits and computer networks must be installed according to government standards. The VDV (video/data/voice) installer technician is also an expert in security and automatic access systems, video installations, and other modern electronic designs.

Those are merely summaries of the job descriptions of electricians. Some specialize within each category. Others perform different types of electrical work.

The Electrician's Personality

Occupational advisers say electricians need to have a realistic personality. What does that mean?

Vocational psychologist John L. Holland developed what are called the Holland Codes to help guide career seekers. He identified six personality types that can help people decide which careers probably suit them best. The Career Key, a career counseling Web site, posted Holland's summary of someone with a realistic personality, including the traits of such a personality. They are the following:

- Likes to work with animals, tools, or machines; generally avoids social activities like teaching, counseling, nursing, and informing others
- Has good skills in working with tools, mechanical drawings, machines, or animals

Electrical skills are needed to maintain all types of machinery that rely on electrical systems, including cars, trucks, and heavy equipment.

- Values practical things you can see and touch—like plants and animals you can grow, or things you can build or make better; and
- Sees self as practical, mechanical, and realistic

Shatkin, in his book *Great Jobs in the President's Stimulus Plan*, notes that "realistic" jobs "frequently involve work activities that include practical, hands-on problems and solutions." People with these jobs don't mind getting dirty.

Tools of the trade for structural electricians: They must know how to use assorted electrical equipment and how to read detailed building plans.

O*NET, a well-known provider of occupational information on the Internet, describes characteristics of the electrician's work style. This type of professional pays attention to detail; demonstrates leadership skills; can take the initiative and work independently; is dependable, cooperative, and honest; can adapt to a variety of workplaces; is a logical, analytical thinker;

A CHANGING PROFESSION

During his thirty-six years as an electrician, Marion Matthews has seen many changes. Most involve computerization. "Technology has come a long way," he says.

Matthews became an electrician's apprentice after serving in the U.S. Navy. "I didn't have any marketable skills," he says. "I'd always wanted to be an electrician. It just amazed me how electrical systems work. To bring power to homes, make lights burn, provide heating—that's what I wanted to do."

His apprenticeship involved on-the-job training and twice-a-week classes. It lasted four years. Afterward, he became a journeyman electrician under union contract. Although he lived in South Carolina, project assignments took him coast to coast. He worked in houses, schools, factories, paper mills, shipping yards, and nuclear power plants. As construction methods and technologies changed, he and his coworkers constantly learned new skills and techniques.

Matthews advises young people not to consider this career path unless they have an aptitude for math and a keen concern for safety. "Electricity is magical, but it can kill you if you aren't careful."

Recently retired, Matthews looks back on his career with deep pride. "It was a good way to make a living, and it's a great field to get into. You help improve other people's lives."

and can handle stress (such as time pressure during power outages and occasional criticism).

TASKS OF AN ELECTRICIAN

The general job description of an electrician is twofold. This professional installs the wiring and electrical fixtures in new structures. The worker also rewires, repairs, and modernizes electrical elements in old buildings and in remodeling projects. Structures are of many different types. They include homes, outbuildings like workshops and detached garages, office buildings, factories, hospitals, college buildings, and military and other government installations. All of them must be wired properly.

The wiring of a new project begins with planning. An electrician or electrical team studies blueprints of the building and makes diagrams of the wiring that is needed. Electricians note where fixtures and outlets are to be installed and how the wiring should be connected.

Electricians then run the necessary cables and wires throughout the facility, including underground cables. They install light fixtures and dimmers, receptacles, and switchboxes. They run connecting wires through wall spaces. They provide special sockets for heavy appliances, such as refrigerators and clothes dryers. The building project may call for yard lights or streetlights to be installed and serviced.

When a power outage occurs, an electrician must find the cause and solve the problem. Under ordinary circumstances, electricians regularly inspect and test electrical installations, checking dial settings and gauge readings. They make sure each system is running safely and requires as little energy and expense as necessary. They troubleshoot and test fuses, circuit breakers, transformers, and the other parts of electrical systems.

There are many types of building projects. Here, an electrician installs a power conduit in a former supermarket that is being remodeled as a department store.

The underlying rule for an electrician is to make sure all work complies with codes and regulations. City, county, state, and national government departments issue codes. Certain industries impose additional standards for electrical work. Regulations vary from state to state around the country. The electrician needs to thoroughly understand the regulations that apply to every project he or she takes on.

Work on-site is only part of a professional electrician's job. Accurate paperwork is required in any business. A solo electrician or the owner of a small company has a business to run. An electrician working in the field must report on every job completed. The electrician's paperwork includes recordkeeping, writing reports, filling out insurance forms, placing equipment orders, and managing the firm's billing and banking.

ON THE JOB

An electrician who is hired to install the wiring in a new

SOME ELECTRICIANS' TASKS ARE DIFFERENT

Jerry Van Liew, an electrician in Charleston, South Carolina, began learning the trade when he was a teenager. During summers, he helped his grandfather. Van Liew's granddad was a residential electrician who wired new homes and home additions and made service calls to older houses. Van Liew, however, took a different career path. He went to work on the electrical staff of the Veterans Administration Hospital in Charleston. In time, he became the hospital's electric shop supervisor.

Why does a hospital need a whole staff of electricians? Electricity is vital at a large facility like the V.A. hospital. It has 117 beds and serves more than forty thousand patients each year. An equipment failure during surgery or while a patient is on life support can be fatal.

"A typical workday for the electricians at our hospital involves mostly upkeep," Van Liew explains. "We have a lot of equipment. It requires daily checks and preventative maintenance."

He shares these examples:

- Checking every item of electrical medical equipment in the operating rooms every day
- Replacing lightbulbs
- Adding electrical sockets, lighting, and special computer jacks in various offices
- Checking fire alarm and nurse call systems
- Maintaining security surveillance systems
- Ensuring that emergency backup generators constantly are in working order
- Maintaining television sets in patients' rooms and lobbies
- Maintaining computers and phone systems at staff workstations

home or commercial building usually begins by studying the builder's blueprints. Blueprints show where everything is supposed to go as the structure is built, including plumbing and wiring. Blueprints indicate the location of the central electrical system controls, wiring circuits, wall sockets and switches, lighting, and major appliance space.

Electricians then begin installing the system, component by component. They use a variety of tools: hand and power saws and drills, wire strippers, conduit benders, cutting devices, pliers, and screwdrivers. After connecting the elaborate scheme of wiring to circuit breakers and transformers, they must test each connection. Testing tools include voltmeters, ammeters, ohmmeters, and other devices.

Electricians who work mainly in larger construction projects (industrial buildings and office complexes) have more heavy-duty electrical components to work with. They pull groups of wires and cables through large conduits that are concealed between walls. Some are trained to install special cables that will bring power to major telecommunications systems.

Typical jobs are different for electricians specializing in maintenance and repair. Their main task is to identify problems and potential trouble spots in older buildings.

A notable difference between installers of new systems and repairers of old ones is the nature of the time pressure. An electrician who wires a new structure works under the schedule of the general contractor. The building goes up methodically; the electrician is called for at certain stages of overall construction.

When a repair professional is needed, on the other hand, the job often is an emergency. An outage may have left a family or business without power. The affected people may include individuals with serious health problems. Businesses may suffer huge financial losses if they can't return to normal quickly. The service professional is expected to arrive as soon as possible and troubleshoot and fix the problem quickly.

An electrician checks the circuit breakers inside an industrial plant. Circuit breakers shut off power to a circuit that becomes overloaded, preventing a possible fire.

The least stressed electrician is the one who performs inspections and maintenance. Inspectors and maintainers usually work under periodic schedules. They can plan their site visits well in advance. Inspectors look for potential problems in electrical equipment and circuitry. Maintenance workers replace aging wires, fuse boxes, circuit breaker boxes, lighting, and other parts of a system before problems occur. Those who work in factories and other large buildings may service motors and heavy equipment. Many large institutions keep electricians on the job around the clock, working in shifts.

Maintenance workers also function as advisers. They show homeowners shortcomings that could lead to problems unless equipment is modernized. They point out to plant managers equipment that is beginning to deteriorate. They explain the dangers and other possible consequences.

All of these electricians are what might be called generalists. Some professionals, on the other hand, prefer to specialize.

chapter 2

A Variety of Electrical Careers

M any building projects call for several electricians—each with a special set of skills. Repair and maintenance projects may also call for specialists. The same electrician who connects the building to an outside power source may not be qualified to set up a computer network among the offices inside. Other specialists might be called on to install a video monitoring system, alarm system, public address system, or home entertainment system. Some of the many types of electrical professionals are described in this chapter.

Electric Meter Installer and Repairer

Power meters automatically record how much electricity a home or business is using. The meter reading determines what the monthly electric bill will be.

Electrical specialists know how to properly install meters outside homes or office/factory buildings, or on connecting power poles. They test the power meters and repair them when necessary.

DANGER

HIGH VOLTAGE
ELECTRICITY

0-30V.DC SUPPLY
PRI.   SEC.

0-15V.DC SUPPLY
PRI.   SEC.

VOLTS

D-C VOLTS

0-30V.DC-15A

A team of electricians test voltage with an ohmmeter in the power center of a factory. They are making sure the wiring and cabling meet safety standards.

VARIABLE DISTRIBUTION

ELECTRICAL ENGINEERING TECHNICIAN

Factories, large commercial operations, and government and private institutions rely on complex power systems. The staff

THE LIFE OF A LINE WORKER

Career prospects are particularly bright for line workers. They are employed by power companies to maintain and repair the grid of cables that transfer electrical current from power plants to neighborhoods and homes. They often are seen at roadsides with their "bucket trucks," working atop power poles.

The invention of power-lift buckets has made the line worker's life easier and safer. In the early years, line workers relied on spiked shoes and safety belts (and no small amount of muscle and acrobatic skill) to climb poles. They still are trained in pole climbing because buckets are not practical in every situation. They must be able to perform physically demanding work at significant heights, often for long periods. Not surprisingly, an essential item of the line worker's equipment is the hard hat. Line workers also know how to install and repair underground power cables. Depending on the task at hand, line workers may work solo or in pairs or crews.

Besides being able to "work with the wires," this professional must be able to operate the truck and each of its devices. The line worker must be skilled in excavating and trenching. Safety training is required. In case of an accident, an injured worker's first source of assistance will likely be a coworker. Line workers are trained in pole-top rescues and other peculiar types of rescue. They can also perform life-saving first aid, including cardiopulmonary resuscitation (CPR).

typically includes an electrical engineering technician. This professional thoroughly understands electrical theory and knows how to keep the combination of electrical machinery and circuits performing satisfactorily. The job may involve regularly testing electrical systems and electrically powered equipment.

ELECTRICAL EQUIPMENT TESTER AND INSPECTOR

Knowledgeable inspectors and testers make sure specific types of electrical systems are working properly. They may be trained in inspecting and testing computer systems, for instance, or broadcast station transmitters, or radar/SONAR devices. Inspectors and testers are also needed in factories. They must be skilled in using special measuring tools.

ELECTRICAL REPAIRER

Companies, industries, powerhouses, and substations rely on complicated electrical installations. Some run heavy electrical equipment. These installations might include electronic transmitters with controls and antennas. Many of the systems operate around the clock. Electrical repairers make sure when a breakdown occurs, it's fixed in very short order.

Industrial repairers troubleshoot problems and make repairs. Even when there is no problem, many companies keep them on staff. They install new electrical products, test old systems, and make any needed adjustments.

POWER LINE INSTALLERS AND REPAIRERS

Where does electricity come from? Homes, offices, and factories do not generate electricity themselves. They draw electrical

An electrical assistant installs a rack that will hold power and com-munication wires. This work is being performed inside a new oil rig.

current from an outside provider. Their electric company has set up a system of regional, area, and neighborhood lines to transmit power to each customer.

Line installers and repairers keep each customer connected to the outside power company. They repair and replace wires and cables for existing customers, and install lines from the street to customer locations. These workers may be employed by the power company or by a separate electrical firm the power company engages to do the work. Some power line workers erect power poles and even transmission towers.

RELATED JOBS

Electricians don't have to be electricians all their lives. Eventually, they might want to find work other than making daily installations and repairs—and they can.

One option is to go into the electrical parts retail business. A professional electrician or home handyman who enters an

Line workers elevated from a bucket truck repair power lines high above the ground. Inventions like the bucket truck make it possible to carry out astonishing tasks.

electrical parts shop expects to deal with a salesperson who knows ohms from amps. An experienced electrician behind the counter is able to "talk shop" comfortably with any customer and ensure consumer satisfaction. That brings customers back—and generates new business by word of mouth from happy buyers.

A different option is teaching. Some professional electricians possess special people skills in addition to their "realistic" get-it-done personalities. They might consider furthering their education and becoming instructors at high schools, vocational institutions, colleges, and other training centers.

JOB CONDITIONS

Just as job types vary, so do working conditions. Electricians in different jobs have different tasks to perform. From time to time, most must work in situations that are unpleasant. They may need to wear protective gear—hard hats, goggles, special shoes and gloves, and earmuffs.

Electrical job sites are both indoors and outside. Electricians frequently have to work in cramped quarters, such as shallow crawl spaces between the ground and the floor of a building. They may have to twist their bodies into awkward positions for long periods.

Besides the expected hazard posed by electrical currents, electricians may also encounter material hazards. Asbestos, for example, was a type of insulation commonly used around heating systems until the late 1900s. Its advantage is that it is heat-resistant, so it can help reduce the risk of fire. Asbestos was phased out of the construction industry after studies linked it to lung disease. However, it is still found in millions of older homes and office buildings. Electricians who repair and inspect wiring in basements and crawl

The weather can cause huge problems for electrical workers. Ice storms in winter, for example, sometimes leave hundreds of thousands of people without power.

spaces may not be aware that they are inhaling microscopic asbestos fibers.

Those who work outdoors, such as power line installers and repairers, have their own worries—particularly the weather. Winter storms bring down trees, power lines, and power poles. Workers face icy elements to restore power to customers as quickly as possible; they know some victims are in life-and-death situations without heat. In the summer, they often toil for hours in sweltering temperatures. Electrical storms pose obvious hazards. Besides electrical shock, workers sometimes are injured in falls and suffer muscle strains.

LOTS OF TERMS TO LEARN

Electricians use a special vocabulary that sounds strange to others. Young people who pursue an electrician's career should expect to master these terms.

"Ampacity," for example, refers to the amount of current that can safely be transferred through a wire, measured in "amperes." A "conductor" is a metal wire or other material through which electrical current flows freely. An "insulator" is the material wrapped around wires to prevent shocks and fires. A "fuse" is a safety device that contains a soft metal connector for an electrical circuit. If too many electrical appliances are plugged into the circuit, the overload will "blow the fuse" and disable the circuit before a fire or other damage results.

Electricians speak of "loads" and "overloads"—the amount of electricity consumed by all the appliances that are connected to a circuit. And when an electrician mentions a "raceway," it has nothing to do with fast cars or motorcycles; it's an enclosure that protects a group of wires.

In most jobs, electricians have a typical workweek. They often have to work overtime, though, and they may be called on at odd hours for emergency service. In wide-scale emergencies like ice storms and hurricanes, they may work for days and nights on end with only brief breaks.

chapter 3

WHAT SKILLS AND SPECIAL KNOWLEDGE ARE REQUIRED?

Terms such as "mechanical," "practical," "realistic," and "problem solver" have been used to describe electricians. But they only hint at the impressive combination of skills, knowledge, and attitude that make a good electrician. An electrician is required to know a lot about a lot of different things. People skills and good judgment also are needed from day to day.

JUST ONE PART OF A CONNECTED STRUCTURE

Charlie Wing has written the book *How Your House Works*. It is a useful introduction for anyone who wants to become an electrician working in homes and office buildings. A professional electrician understands not just how a building is wired but how it is put together and how the other systems work. A mistake by an electrician can have a bad effect on everything from the furnace to the hot-water heater to the garbage disposal to the icemaker.

Electricians need to have a general understanding of building construction. They should know the qualities of different building materials. Especially, they should automatically recognize materials that are flammable or that pose chemical hazards.

They must understand home and office design. Electricians consult building blueprints and draw their own wiring circuit schematics. Their wiring has to conform to the overall blueprint; architects don't design buildings around the electrical circuitry.

ELECTRICAL SMARTS

Obviously, an electrician must thoroughly understand every aspect of installations and repairs. The student or apprentice will learn

An instructor watches an electrical engineering student draw a circuit diagram on a whiteboard. Electricians must understand how to wire a building effectively and safely.

about the types of electrical current. Power measurements (volts, amps, watts, ohms) will become as simple to interpret as a breakfast menu. Electricians know why different types and sizes of wires and cables are needed for specific purposes. They know how much power various types of electric motors need.

Most important, they understand safety practices. (The first safety rule is to disconnect the current before working on an electrical circuit or component. Touching a "live wire" can shock and even electrocute the worker. Proper grounding is also essential to prevent electrical disasters.) They must be able to spot fire hazards instantly.

Careerists do not need a college degree to become "electrically smart" and safety-minded. They do need one academic strength, though: a good understanding of math. In order to advance in their careers, electricians must understand not only basic arithmetic but also geometry, algebra, calculus, and statistics.

Electricians rewire a home as part of a remodeling project to make it more wheelchair friendly for a resident. Some rewiring tasks are basic, whereas others are very complicated.

A "REALIST" AND A "THINKER"

While electricians should have what career counselors call "realistic" personalities, they need additional personal skills. Foremost, they need to be good thinkers.

Many electrical tasks and problems are simple to deal with: installing a ceiling fan, replacing a burnt fuse, etc. Others are much more difficult. Why does an electrical circuit in a home seem to regularly overload? Are too many appliances being used in one room on the circuit? Or is there a defective socket or wiring? The electrician gathers all of the information about the problem from every source available. The worker considers the possibilities and decides on the first, best approach to solving the problem. This often calls for good judgment as well as experience and knowledge.

"PEOPLE" PROFESSIONALS

Electricians must know how to relate to other people. They don't have to be particularly gifted with the social communication skills that are necessary for teachers, lawyers, and salespeople. However, electricians do interact with their customers, bosses, and assistants every day. They need to use proper English and communicate effectively. Those who run their own businesses must be leaders who can coordinate the assignments of their workers. They should be able to communicate effectively in person, by phone, by text message, or by e-mail.

They must be good listeners. When a customer, colleague, or supervisor speaks, the electrician should focus on what is being said. It is vital to completely understand the problem or assignment at hand. The professional should ask questions and consider others' suggestions as to the cause and solutions.

Electricians develop a "sixth sense" in their work. As they explore a job site, they learn to detect problems and potential problems that are not obvious at first glance. O*NET, the online provider of occupational information, calls this trait "problem sensitivity."

O*NET points out that an electrician needs good "deductive reasoning" and "inductive reasoning" powers. Deductive reasoning is "the ability to apply general rules to specific problems to produce answers that make sense." Inductive reasoning combines bits of information "to form general rules or conclusions"; this "includes finding a relationship among seemingly unrelated events."

The electrician might be called to a home where an electrical circuit has been disabled. Checking records, the electrician sees that a problem with this circuit has occurred the past two years—at approximately the same time of the same month. As it turns out, that is the time of year when the family has numerous relatives in town for a weekend. Two hair dryers are turned on at the same time in the guest bathroom. Other current-drawing devices are used simultaneously in guest bedrooms—all on the same circuit. The electrician can explain to the homeowner how to remedy the problem by taking turns using appliances.

As the electrician gains experience, knowledge accumulates. The electrician learns to weigh the strengths and risks of different approaches that could be taken in any given situation. Time turns apprentice and journeyman electricians into master electricians—"experts."

PHYSICAL REQUIREMENTS

Electricians need to be in good condition generally. Their work is often physically demanding.

An electrician tests the current in a wiring system. Color-coding identifies different types of wires and connections, greatly simplifying such work.

Keen eyesight is vital. One reason is that electrical wires are color-coded. Another is that sharp near vision can mean the difference between a successful job and calamity. Electricians frequently find themselves studying wire connections from a distance of only a few inches.

Good eye-hand coordination and manual dexterity are essential as well. The worker must be able to move hands and arms quickly and work nimbly with fingers and thumbs. The electrician regularly must grasp and manipulate tools, wires, and other objects. Situations become weird, at times. After a few minutes at an awkward body angle under a crawl space, the worker may want to adjust the body position while keeping a grip on the pliers or screwdriver.

Finger dexterity likewise is crucial. Many types of electrical screws are tiny. Capping or splicing procedures often involve delicate wire ends.

Indoors or out, the work sometimes is strenuous. Electricians may have to lift and carry heavy equipment. They may work at heights, standing on ladders or scaffolds. They have to crawl on hands and knees and crouch in uncomfortable positions—sometimes for extended periods of time—as they install, replace, and repair wiring, fixtures, and other items. They need an excellent sense of balance.

TOOLS OF THE ELECTRICIAN'S TRADE

An electrician must be good with tools and mechanics. Every utility professional knows the secret of success is in having the right tools for the job—and knowing how to use them. Besides screwdrivers and wire cutters, what items might be found in the electrician's toolkit?

Stripping devices. These include sharp grips that can strip synthetic insulation off bare wires (in order to make new connections) and other implements.

Measuring and testing devices. Electricians frequently bring out their ohmmeters, ammeters, milliammeters, voltmeters, test lamps, oscilloscopes, and other equipment to check current, intensity, etc. Their main

concern is to be sure the electrical system or machine is functioning safely.

Power tools. It often is necessary to use saws, drills, and other power tools to perform an electrical installation or get to a behind-the-wall electrical problem.

Electricians may use thousands of feet of wires and cables on a construction project. Here, an electrician unwinds reels of wire at a work site.

Wire and cable reels. A variety of reels and related devices make it easy to contain and dispense lengths of wires and outside cables.

Computer software. Everyday life has become heavily computerized. Software engineers have devised programs to help electricians perform their tasks. Analytical software helps electricians evaluate electrical and lighting installations. Architectural and design programs help them plan and diagram a new electrical installation throughout a building. Project management and database software helps them make precise job estimates and keep accurate records.

Besides knowing how to use their special tools and equipment, electricians should be able to repair them. This can save them a lot of money. If they're in the middle of a job, an on-the-spot repair—even it it's only a temporary fix—can save them a significant amount of time.

chapter 4

WHAT TRAINING IS REQUIRED?

Electrical apprentices in the United States must have a high school diploma or General Equivalency Diploma (GED). They must be at least eighteen years old. Some may need to take additional math classes before they're accepted into an apprenticeship program.

Training programs for electricians involve both classroom instruction and on-the-job work supervised by professional electricians. A post–high school apprenticeship program may take four years and require up to two thousand on-the-job hours in addition to 144 course hours. In most scenarios, the trainee then must obtain a license by passing an exam. The applicant must demonstrate a working knowledge of electrical theory and an understanding of national and local codes—particularly, the National Electrical Code (NEC).

According to the BLS, "Most electricians acquire their skills by completing an apprenticeship program lasting four to five years." Apprenticeships include both classroom instruction and on-the-job training. Training committees might consist of members of the International Brotherhood of Electrical Workers union, the National Electrical Contractors Association, other electrical associations, and local electrical company professionals.

The National Joint Apprenticeship and Training Committee (NJATC) offers apprentice training, journeyman training, and

Speed is vital in rescuing an injured line worker. Journeyman and apprentice electricians compete in rescue drills at the annual International Lineman's Rodeo and Expo.

instructor courses at training centers throughout the United States and Canada. The National Electrical Contractors Association and the International Brotherhood of Electrical Workers develop the courses. Apprentice training is provided for those who want to become outside linemen, inside wiremen (commercial and industrial buildings), residential wiremen, and VDV installer technicians. Journeyman courses teach new skills to veteran electricians as new technologies are developed. Advanced training is available for qualified electrical instructors.

Government agencies and higher learning facilities also offer apprenticeship programs. The government regulates the apprenticeship system. The U.S. Department of Labor oversees a Bureau of Apprenticeship and Training. Apprentices are employed under contract, based on the National Apprenticeship Act of 1937. Trade unions regulate apprenticeships in some states.

EARNING WHILE LEARNING

Apprentice electricians are paid during their training time. The definition of "apprentice" has changed over the centuries. During the Middle Ages, an apprentice was a child or teenager taken under the wing of a skilled craftsman or tradesman. The young person received room and board but no (or very little) pay. An apprentice performed the dull "dirty work" in the master's shop, while watching the master work and learning skills. The master, in turn, obtained very cheap assistance.

Today, in electrical and other career fields, an apprentice is more like a rookie employee. The apprentice electrician works for a licensed electrician—for pay—as an assistant and learner. It's the "earn as you learn" principle.

The *Occupational Outlook Handbook* observes, "Because of the comprehensive training received, those who complete apprenticeship programs qualify to do both maintenance and construction work."

Entering the profession as an apprentice is a career investment. In time, the apprentice becomes a journeyman—a professional.

Students can find information about apprenticeships and other electrician job opportunities at their state employment

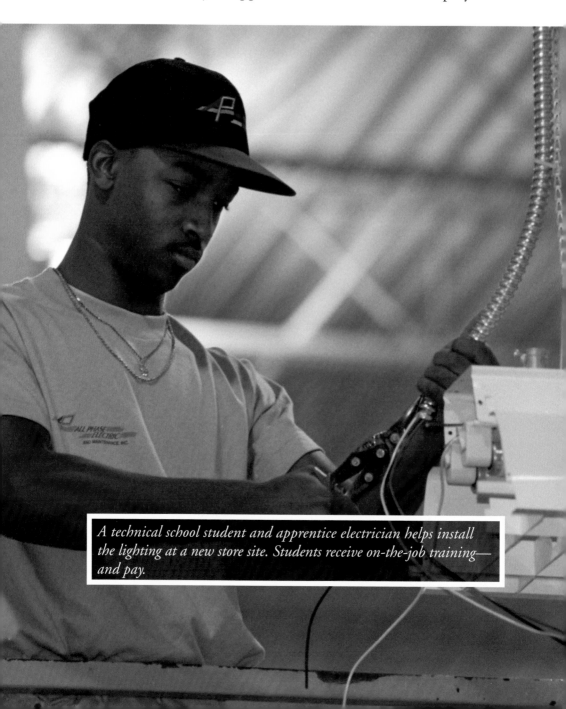

A technical school student and apprentice electrician helps install the lighting at a new store site. Students receive on-the-job training—and pay.

offices or apprenticeship agencies. Local electricians can provide details. Students can also call the U.S. Department of Labor for apprenticeship information, at (877) 872-5627. Additional sources of guidance include the Independent Electrical Contractors, the National Electrical Contractors Association, the Associated Builders and Contractors, the International Brotherhood of Electrical Workers union, and the Home Builders Institute. (See "For More Information" in the back of this book for contact information for these organizations.)

TRAINING FOR GENERAL ELECTRICIANS

Michael Farr, in his book *300 Best Jobs Without a Four-Year Degree*, describes the skills an electrician must master and the basic course subjects that are required. Skills are in these areas:

- Installation of equipment and wiring to specifications
- Use of specific tools to repair equipment and electrical systems

- Ability to troubleshoot problems—to find the causes and determine the best solutions
- Ability to maintain equipment, keeping it in safe working order
- Equipment and technology design and selection— deciding what equipment and tools are necessary for a job, and adapting them to provide satisfactory service
- Operations analysis and monitoring—determining the requirements for an electrical project and, after installation, checking to ensure it is functioning properly
- Financial management— getting the best value for money spent on an electrical project, and keeping accurate records on expenses

Course subjects, Farr explains, include the following:

Building and construction. The student learns about materials, methods, and tools that are required for the construction and repair of buildings, streets, and other structures.

Mechanics. An electrician must be familiar with the use, design,

and maintenance of tools and equipment that are used on the job.

Design. An electrical student examines building blueprints, plans, and design sketches and models, and learns about the structural design process.

A student learns the workings of electrical transformers under the instruction of a professional. Trainees must take classes in many related topics, including construction, design, and physics.

Production and processing of materials. Electricians must be familiar with raw material production, quality-control issues, costs, etc.

Physics. Physical principles affect most aspects of electricians' work—electrical, mechanical, material, and more.

Personal skills. A successful electrician must be able to ensure customer satisfaction. This involves understanding the customer's needs, providing quality service, and evaluating customer satisfaction after the project is completed.

The BLS, in its *Occupational Outlook Handbook*, describes apprentice education as follows: "In the classroom, apprentices learn electrical theory, blueprint reading, mathematics, electrical code requirements, and safety and first-aid practices. They also may receive specialized training in soldering, communications, fire alarm systems, and cranes and elevators.

"On the job, apprentices work under the supervision of experienced electricians. At first, they drill holes, set anchors, and attach conduit. Later, they measure, fabricate, and install conduit and install, connect, and test wiring, outlets, and switches. They also learn to set up and draw diagrams for entire electrical systems. Eventually, they practice and master all of an electrician's main tasks."

TRAINING FOR RELATED AND SPECIALTY CAREERS

Students who want to work in related or specialty fields may need to enroll in programs focused on a variety of other subjects. These might include computer technology, industrial electronics, electromechanical and instrumentation technology, power transmission installation, line work, or quality control. Certain programs may require courses in topics such as mechanics, physics, home design, and customer service.

Here are some examples of training programs required for related professionals:

- Electric meter installer and repairer. Electromechanics, electrical instrumentation, and electrical maintenance technology.
- Electrical engineering technician. Electrical/electronic engineering technology, computer systems technology, computer engineering technology, telecommunications technology, and various electronic or communications engineering programs.
- Electrical equipment tester and inspector. Electrical or technological quality control.
- Electrical repairer. Industrial electronics technology, and computer installation and service. (Job prospects are best if the applicant has an associate's degree in electronics.)
- Power line installer and repairer. Power transmission installation, line work, and electrical and power transmission and installation.

Many power companies collaborate with technical schools to provide training for line workers. One example is York Technical College in Rock Hill, South Carolina, which offers certificate courses as well as associate's degree programs. The entry-level line worker certificate program includes nine weeks of classroom, laboratory, and field training. Students learn to climb poles and install power lines overhead and underground. They are also taught safety regulations. After completion, the power company that hires them provides extensive additional training, both on the job and in the classroom.

LEARNING "THE CODE"

The basic codebook for electricians is the NEC. The National Electrical Contractors Association calls it the "bedrock of the electrical construction business." It is revised every three years. Changes are based on new information and recommendations from professional electricians, consumers, product manufacturers, inspectors, and others. The National Fire Protection Association (NFPA) publishes the NEC. It is more than seven hundred pages long, and electricians are advised to become very familiar with its contents. Electrical companies and unions frequently teach classes on NEC changes for their employees.

The NEC is not an instruction book. It is not intended to teach electricians how to do their work. Its purpose is to ensure that all of their installations, upgrades, and repairs are performed according to proven safety standards.

The NEC is not "the law," either. The NFPA cannot enforce it. State and local governments, though, base their wiring regulations on the NEC. If new electrical installations do not meet NEC standards, power companies usually will refuse to connect raw power to the building. Insurance companies will

TOUGH QUESTIONS

Students in electrical programs must learn details about terms that are alien to most people: "overcurrent," "grounding conductor," "ampacity," "correction factors." Ordinary citizens don't want or need to understand what they mean. They expect their electricians, though, to understand them perfectly and ensure efficient, safe work.

The Construction Craft Training Center (CCTC) offers a program for electrical trainees in California. It is one of many training institutions for electricians throughout the country. Sample questions in one of its online practice exams, Journeyman Exam 1, include the following:

1. The branch circuit conductor supplying a 3/4 hp, 1Ø 115-volt motor shall have an ampacity of at least _____.
2. How many #1 wires can you install in parallel?
3. What is the minimum number of 20 amp branch circuits required for a 1,500 square-foot house?
4. The overcurrent protection of a #10 THW conductor, when there are not more than three conductors in a raceway, and the ambient temperature is 28°C, would be _____ amps.
5. You are wiring a house that has 2,200 square feet under the roof. The living area accounts for 2,000 square feet of this space. The minimum general lighting load for this dwelling would be _____ VA.
6. What size dual-element fuse does the Code require for a 2 hp, 208-volt, single-phase motor?
7. The correction factor (C.F.) for 104°F is ____ for a 60°C insulated conductor.
8. When sizing the service conductors for an apartment complex, the minimum demand load in kW for eight 4 kW ranges would be ____kW.
9. What is the minimum size copper equipment grounding conductor required for a 80 amp circuit breaker?
10. The branch-circuit protection for a 1Ø, 115v, 3 hp motor would normally be ____ using dual element time delay fuses.

Happily, the answers are multiple-choice.

contest damage or injury claims that could have resulted from faulty wiring. They may refuse to insure the facility altogether unless the electrical work conforms with the NEC.

Other standards used by electricians include Building Officials and Code Administrators (BOCA) guides and the International Residential Code (IRC). Electricians must comply with federal Occupational Safety and Health Administration (OSHA) standards. Some state and local regulations impose additional requirements for electrical work.

The National Electrical Contractors Association (NECA) publishes its own set of codes, the National Electrical Installation Standards (NEIS). According to the NECA, they "go beyond the minimum safety requirements of the National Electrical Code." Their intent is to ensure that electrical products and systems are installed in a "neat and workmanlike manner." The association explains, "With NEIS, the electrical installation you design or install not only meets code—it meets the shared expectations of everyone involved: owner, specifying engineer, electrical contractor, and the authority having jurisdiction."

LEARNING ON THE JOB, LEARNING IN CLASS

Some young people are interested in electrical occupations, but they are not ready to commit to a lengthy apprentice program. For their first step, they might obtain jobs as electricians' helpers. Rather than performing electrical work, they can be useful in preparing work sites, running errands, helping gather and transport material, etc. As they observe electricians and apprentices on the job, they may decide it isn't for them—or they may quickly be convinced that it is.

On the other hand, some electrical students decide to complete much or most of their classroom study before they become on-the-job apprentices. Many vocational and technical institutions offer courses. The *Occupational Outlook Handbook* points out, "Employers often hire students who complete these programs and usually start them at a more advanced level than those without this training."

The Internet has made online learning opportunities available to millions of people who can't enroll in classes at a physical college campus. Some institutions offer study-at-home training for aspiring electricians. One is Penn Foster Career School in Scranton, Pennsylvania (http://www.pennfoster.edu/electrician).

Penn Foster has career school diploma programs for electricians, basic electronics trainees, and electronics technicians. The electricians program teaches such subjects as electricity classifications and categories; conduit fittings and supports; the installation of residential, commercial, and industrial electrical components; heating and lighting methods; and the properties of electrical conductors.

Note that students who successfully complete the programs are not yet authorized to enter the workplace as electrical and electronic service professionals. They must pass the required testing for certification, such as the Electronics Technicians Association Certification Exam, and acquire on-the-job training. Penn Foster's programs include exam preparation.

Penn Foster offers an associate's degree in electrical engineering technology. Studying at home, students take courses in such subjects as fundamentals of electricity, electrical and electronic measurement and instruments, and electric motors and controls. They ultimately work in the business sector, manufacturing, or government agencies.

The institution has an associate's degree program in electronics technology. Students learn electronics fundamentals, electronic instrumentation and measurement, the testing of circuits and electronic components, and industrial electronics. They may go to work for an electronics repair business.

chapter 5

BEGINNING AND ADVANCING IN AN ELECTRICAL CAREER

After completing high school and basic instruction courses, the career electrician begins by obtaining on-the-job training. Ideally, this can be accomplished as part of an apprenticeship program. High school and vocational technology instructors can point students to internship and apprenticeship training programs in the area—and to prospective employers.

With or without the aid of vocational career counselors, an aspiring electrician is a job seeker. Job seekers in any career area should develop a résumé at an early age. A résumé is the document that tells potential employers about the applicant's educational background, work experience, and unique skills. For the rest of their active careers, workers should update their résumés as they acquire new skills and advance in their jobs. The longer a person works, the longer and more impressive the résumé will become.

LICENSING

With training completed, an electrician must become licensed. Requirements for a license differ among states, but certain fundamental knowledge is the same everywhere. Applicants

GETTING A START WITH JOB CORPS

Job Corps is a U.S. Department of Labor program that educates and trains at-risk young people. The Home Builders Institute (HBI), part of the National Association of Home Builders, partners with Job Corps to train young workers in residential construction. Among other trades, the HBI and Job Corps offer a program in electrical wiring. Its purpose is to provide basic, on-the-job skills to students who want to become electricians.

Students who enroll in the program can learn at their own pace. The average completion time is one year. A graduate from the program probably can obtain an entry-level job that pays a little above the minimum wage. However, the real goal is to use this training as a stepping-stone toward a professional career.

The HBI suggests a career choice "ladder" for an electrical wiring graduate that climbs in this way: electrician helper, electrician apprentice, journeyman electrician, job superintendent, electrical supply manager, electrical inspector, electrical engineer, and general electric contractor. Some jobs, the HBI points out, "require years of experience in the trade, and, in some cases, further education. Additional training through apprenticeships or on-the-job training will upgrade your skills and help expand your career options."

have to prove they thoroughly understand electrical theory and know the NEC. They also must know the requirements of the electrical and building codes imposed by their local government agencies.

Additional licensing may be required for electrical contractors who bid on public projects. For example, they may need to be licensed as master electricians. Master electricians are veteran electricians with at least seven years of experience; many have electrical engineering degrees.

Ironically, many consumers don't care whether an electrician is licensed or not. A survey in Ontario, Canada, in 2009 indicated that 70 percent of citizens were willing to hire unqualified friends, relatives, or neighbors to install light fixtures if it would save them money. Almost half of those surveyed would let amateurs install electrical outlets and light timers. Forty-five percent said they didn't bother to verify if an electrician was licensed.

In most places, offering commercial electrician services without a license is illegal—for good reason. Lucy Impera, a licensing official with Ontario's Electrical Safety Authority, worries that many consumers "don't understand the seriousness of electrical hazards." She points out that even though an installation seems to work properly, the situation behind the wall could be unsafe. In time, fire or electrocution could result.

A reel of coaxial cable is installed underground at a school construction site. Almost 15,000 feet (4,572 meters) of heavy cable was required for this project.

In Ontario alone, more than a hundred people have been electrocuted in the past ten years, and more than thirty-three thousand electrical fires have been recorded. Impera urges customers to be sure they are hiring a licensed electrician. After the job is completed, she adds, they should arrange for an electrical inspector to examine the workmanship.

ADVANCEMENT PATHS

It is a wonderful accomplishment to obtain an electrician's license. Education and testing never end, though. Professionals

LEARNING FROM A RELATIVE

Some young people have a special advantage when it comes to investigating a career as an electrician: a relative who's already in the business. A parent, grandparent, or other relative can not only be an inspiration but also a valuable trainer.

"In high school, I took vocational training in AC and refrigeration, where I learned some basic electricity and control wiring," says Jerry Van Liew, the hospital electrical supervisor in Charleston, South Carolina. "But most of my early training came from helping my grandfather every summer. He was a licensed electrician who did mostly residential wiring and service calls.

"You can work as an electrician with any electrical contractor in residential or commercial wiring. But to work for yourself, you must have a license, which requires learning the National Electric Code book and taking a state test. Many electrical companies also offer electrician helpers the opportunity to attend apprenticeship classes, which can last from two to four years. Upon completion, you can get your journeyman's license."

must keep their licenses current. They may need additional courses from time to time concerning new types of electrical systems.

Meanwhile, professional electricians must stay abreast of changes in building codes and license requirements. They enroll in safety classes. Manufacturers of electrical products often provide training for their electrician customers. Electrical contractors, or electricians who wish to become contractors, can benefit from business and management courses.

Advancement in the electrical professions is based on increasing experience. It is also affected by the changing workplace.

The BLS reports that almost 70 percent of electricians work for construction contractors. About 11 percent are self-employed. The other 20 percent are maintenance electricians in various industries. Many young people who are considering

A fire investigator takes photos at the scene of a home fire. It was determined that the fire was caused by a faulty electrical connection in the living room ceiling fan.

a career as an electrician assume they will begin by working under experienced professionals, but eventually will start their own business.

The *Occupational Outlook Handbook* points to other advancement paths, such as the job of electrical supervisor. Experienced electricians who have years of experience in construction might diversify and become construction superintendents or project managers. Major building projects can be both residential (multihome neighborhoods) and commercial/industrial. Some project managers and superintendents who have shrewd business and management skills decide to launch their own contracting businesses.

General electricians can advance by becoming specialists. A different advancement opportunity is to become an electrical inspector for an industry, government agency, or consulting firm. All electricians can tell if a basic installation or electrical item meets safety standards; an inspector has further expertise to spot hazards and regulation violations that are not so obvious.

A Bonus for Workers and Supervisors Alike: Bilingual Skills

The BLS has observed that Spanish-speaking workers represent large segments of construction workers in many regions of the United States. "For those who seek to advance," the BLS reports in its *Occupational Outlook Handbook*, "it is increasingly important to be able to communicate in both English and Spanish in order to relay instructions and safety precautions to workers with limited understanding of English."

At the same time, it notes, "Spanish-speaking workers who want to advance in this occupation need very good

English skills to understand electrician classes and installation instructions, which are usually written in English and are highly technical."

ELECTRICAL SERVICE IS A BUSINESS

Starting a business is not the difficult part. Some solo electricians operate out of small shops at their homes. Others lease or

This former electrician has found a profitable new career making rooftop solar installations. The growing use of alternative energy sources is expanding job possibilities for electricians.

buy separate facilities. The great challenge is not to start the business but to build a successful business once it's begun.

Electricians who work for themselves must have a keen business sense. By practicing economy and managing resources wisely, electricians can minimize their costs and thus attract new customers. Electrical contractors and individual electricians need to know who the most economical suppliers are—big-box chains as well as locally owned parts stores. They must determine how money will be spent to get the work done, and they must account for expenditures. To make a good profit, they must be able to closely estimate how long it will take to perform a job and what it will cost.

They must also understand the importance of customer relations. The electrician should be able to explain to customers exactly what work is being performed, in language the average person can understand. Not only do electricians need to know what they're doing, but they also need to assure customers that they know what they're doing.

chapter 6

FUTURE PROSPECTS FOR ELECTRICIANS

The BLS predicts continued job growth for electricians at least through 2016. In its *Occupational Outlook Handbook, 2008–09 Edition*, it projects: "As the population and economy grow, more electricians will be needed to install and maintain electrical devices and wiring in homes, factories, offices, and other structures. An increase in power plant construction over the next ten years will require many additional electricians. New technologies also are expected to continue to spur demand for these workers. For example, buildings increasingly need wiring to accommodate computers and telecommunications equipment. Robots and other automated manufacturing systems in factories also will require the installation and maintenance of more complex wiring systems. As the economy rehabilitates and retrofits older structures, which usually require electrical improvements to meet modern codes, it will create additional jobs."

Related career fields are also expected to expand. For example, Michael Farr and Laurence Shatkin, in *225 Best Jobs for Baby Boomers*, project almost ninety thousand job openings each year for electrical and electronic inspectors and testers.

Career prospects are especially bright for line workers hired by power companies. Between 2007 and 2012, some thirty thousand line-worker jobs may need to be filled, according to the Center for Energy Workforce Development. That represents approximately half of the workforce of skilled line workers.

There are several reasons for the need for young line workers. Older workers are retiring, and a growing population is creating more energy demands. Energy companies must build new power plants. Regardless of the raw energy sources they use (coal, nuclear, water, solar), providers convert energy to electricity. This calls for expanded electrical distribution systems.

A power company invests considerable money and time in training employees on the job. Naturally, it wants to retain its experienced workers for many years. This means line workers can expect good pay and job benefits, as well as continuing education and steadily improving work conditions.

While new work and additional jobs for electricians are expected to increase, old jobs are being vacated as veteran

A worker helps install electrical wiring underground. The wires will convey electrical power harnessed by wind turbines to a wind energy plant.

electricians retire. This creates job openings for new electricians each year.

NOT ALL TIMES ARE GOOD TIMES

Even solid career paths sometimes have their ups and downs. Throughout 2008 and 2009, a slump in building construction resulted in a downturn for electricians who specialized in new electrical installations. Other types of electrical services also were badly affected by the recession. In Chicago, Illinois, for instance, the Metropolitan Pier and Exposition Authority had to restructure its management and maintenance staff. The organization oversees conventions and trade shows at McCormick Place and Navy Pier. As convention and show activity declined, it let go a hundred of its electricians.

A REWARDING CAREER

Jerry Van Liew, the hospital electrician in Charleston, loves his job. "I've been doing electrical work for twenty-eight years and find it to be a very rewarding career. The satisfaction for me is knowing everything in our facility is working, and our patients and staff are happy."

The work requires constant alertness, though. "The thing I don't like is working on live electrical circuits, which can be hazardous if you are not a trained, qualified electrician," he says.

Still, he recommends an electrician career for any young person who has a mind for solving problems. By making sure electrical systems are reliable and safe, electricians perform a tremendous service to society.

Van Liew agrees it is a "recession-proof" career path. "There will always be a need for electricians," he says.

Nationwide, all workers on new construction projects, including electricians, are affected by economic changes. "Workers in these trades may experience periods of unemployment when the overall level of construction falls," the *Occupational Outlook Handbook* states. "On the other hand, shortages of these workers may occur in some areas during peak periods of building activity."

An eventual building rebound is expected to return construction to a bustling rate of activity. The BLS says electrician jobs will vary by specialty and location. Prospects are best in "the fastest growing regions of the country, especially those areas where power plants are being constructed."

There will always be a steady need for electricians to make repairs and modernize the electrical systems in existing structures. The Department of Labor confirms that "employment of maintenance electricians is steadier than that of construction electricians." On the other hand, "those working in the automotive and other manufacturing industries that are sensitive to cyclical swings in the economy may experience layoffs during recessions. In addition, opportunities for maintenance electricians may be limited in many industries by the increased contracting out for electrical services in an effort to reduce operating costs."

A TWENTY-FIRST CENTURY SPECIALTY: DIGITAL WIRING

The use of personal computers and the Internet has increased at an explosive rate during the past twenty-five years. Home and office consumers want the latest and greatest digital products. These include state-of-the-art entertainment systems, video-conferencing systems, advanced computer networks, surveillance and alarm systems, and backup power systems that will keep their equipment running whenever normal power is interrupted.

It may look like a mess at the moment, but this skilled residential electrician soon will have the wires connected safely in a new home's breaker box.

Some avid technology buffs have begun using their home PCs as "control centers." Their computers can monitor and adjust almost everything electrical in the home or office: the temperature, the on-off patterns of indoor lights and outdoor floodlights, the movement of track lights, security cameras in different areas, the coffeemaker, the Crock-Pot, the clothes dryer, etc.

Dennis C. Brewer, a network engineer, and Paul A. Brewer, an electrical engineer and master electrician, observe, "In the twenty-first century, digital lifestyles will influence home design as never before. The modern home is a place for high-fidelity entertainment, advanced communications, and automated convenience." That means modern wiring projects may involve "whole-home remote controls, cable TV systems, computer networks, public address systems, multi-room sound, back-up power, and the latest phone systems." Such wiring may extend outside to decks, the poolside, and outbuildings.

Electricians who learn how to wire homes and offices to meet the new demands of the digital generation have an advantage in marketing their services.

SPECIALIST, JACK-OF-ALL-TRADES— TAKE YOUR CHOICE

Although some electricians—beginners and veterans—will choose to specialize, experts say future job prospects are best for electricians who have multiple skills. As predicted above, they are especially promising for experts in modern computer electronics—electricians who can effectively wire video and audio systems and advanced data networks. But the outlook is also bright for a professional who can perform many types of tasks at the same job site.

Throughout the United States and Canada, young people are eyeing careers as electricians. The work is intriguing and challenging, and it will always be in demand.

glossary

academic Pertaining to school studies.

analytical Requiring a problem to be separated into parts to find a solution.

blueprint A print of a technical drawing with white lines printed on a blue background, or a print with blue lines on a white background, usually of an architectural or engineering design.

cardiopulmonary resuscitation (CPR) The emergency treatment of a person whose heart has stopped beating.

circuit A wiring system that supplies a group of outlets with power.

circuit breaker A device that automatically opens (disables) an electrical circuit when it becomes overloaded.

codes A set of rules and requirements.

component A part.

conduit A protective, nonmetallic sleeve or "raceway" through which electrical wires are run.

consumer A buyer and user of a product or service.

dexterity The easy use of hands, arms, and legs.

digital The functioning of a device (such as a computer) by numerical units.

electrocution Death by electrical shock.

flammable Easy to ignite.

grounding Returning electrical current to earth.

insulation Material that prevents an electrical wire or cable from causing a shock or fire.

preventative maintenance Electrical replacement or upgrading done for the purpose of avoiding future disasters.

radar An electronic system that uses radio waves to detect and identify distant objects.

receptacle A mounted electrical fitting that contains the live parts of a circuit.

regulations Rules established by a government agency or other legal authority.

résumé A short summary of a person's educational and work experience.

schematic The diagram of an electrical system.

SONAR An underwater electronic detection system.

standards A body of procedures and rules that have become accepted over time.

telecommunications Communications over long distances by telephones, now expanded by the Internet and satellite systems.

transformer An electrical component that alters voltage levels.

utility Electrical, plumbing, heating, or a similar service that provides daily needs.

videoconferencing People in distant locations meeting online, in real time, via computers and the Internet.

for more information

Associated Builders and Contractors
4250 North Fairfax Drive, 9th Floor
Arlington, VA 22203-1607
(703) 812-2000
Web site: http://www.abcr.org
This association of construction firms provides a network for
    apprentice and student training.

Bureau of Labor Statistics
U.S. Department of Labor
2 Massachusetts Avenue NE, Suite 2135
Washington, DC 20212-0001
(202) 691-5700
Web site: http://www.bls.gov
Each year, the BLS updates the *Occupational Outlook
    Handbook*, which describes thousands of careers with
    details about job requirements and average salaries.

Electrical Safety Authority
155A Matheson Boulevard W, Suite 202
Mississauga, ON L5R 3L5
Canada
(905) 712-5696
Web site: http://www.esasafe.com
This nonprofit organization is responsible for public electrical
    safety in Ontario.

Employment and Training Administration
U.S. Department of Labor
Frances Perkins Building

200 Constitution Avenue NW
Washington, DC 20210
Web site: http://www.doleta.gov
ETA training information includes links to state apprenticeship
    Web sites (http://www.doleta.gov/OA/sainformation.cfm).

Home Builders Institute
1201 Fifteenth Street NW, 6th Floor
Washington, DC 20005
(800) 795-7955
Web site: http://www.hbi.org
This organization works to advance training and education to
    those in the housing industry.

Independent Electrical Contractors
4401 Ford Avenue, Suite 1100
Alexandria, VA 22302
(703) 549-7351
Web site: http://www.ieci.org
This national trade organization provides electrical contrac-
    tors with educational programs, services, and products.

International Brotherhood of Electrical Workers
900 Seventh Street NW
Washington, DC 20001
(202) 833-7000
Web site: http://www.ibew.org
This is the world's largest electrical union.

National Association of Home Builders
1201 Fifteenth Street NW
Washington, DC 20005
(800) 368-5242
Web site: http://www.nahb.org

This trade association promotes legislative, regulatory, and
judicial policies affecting home builders.

National Electrical Contractors Association
3 Bethesda Metro Center, Suite 1100
Bethesda, MD 20814
(301) 657-3110
Web site: http://www.necanet.org
This organization is the national voice of the electrical contracting industry.

National Fire Protection Association
1 Batterymarch Park
Quincy, MA 02169-7471
(617) 770-3000
Web site: http://www.nfpa.org
The NFPA publishes the National Electrical Code.

National Joint Apprenticeship Training Committee
301 Prince George's Boulevard
Upper Marlboro, MD 20774
(301) 715-2300
Web site: http://www.njatc.org
This national organization develops and standardizes training
for electricians.

WEB SITES

Due to the changing nature of Internet links, Rosen Publishing
has developed an online list of Web sites related to the subject
of this book. This site is updated regularly. Please use this link
to access the list:

http://www.rosenlinks.com/ecar/elec

for further reading

Apel, Melanie Ann. *Careers in the Building and Construction Trades* (Careers in the New Economy). New York, NY: Rosen Publishing Group, Inc., 2005.

Bolles, Richard Nelson, et al. *What Color Is Your Parachute? For Teens: Discovering Yourself, Defining Your Future.* Berkeley, CA: Ten Speed Press, 2006.

Brickner, C. Dale, and John E Traister. *Electrician's Exam Preparation Guide.* Carlsbad, CA: Craftsman Book Company, 2008.

Byers, Ann. *Great Résumé, Application, and Interview Skills* (Work Readiness). New York, NY: Rosen Publishing Group, Inc., 2008.

Casio, Jim, and Alice Rush. *Green Careers: Choosing Work for a Sustainable Future.* Gabriola Island, BC: New Society Publishers, 2009.

Farndon, Don. *Electricity: An Investigation* (Science Investigations). New York, NY: Rosen Publishing Group, Inc., 2008.

Ferguson, Dave. *Construction* (Discovering Careers for Your Future). 2nd ed. New York, NY: Chelsea House, 2008.

Gibilisco, Stan. *Teach Yourself Electricity and Electronics.* 4th ed. New York, NY: McGraw-Hill, 2006.

Harmon, Daniel E. *First Job Smarts* (Get Smart with Your Money). New York, NY: Rosen Publishing Group, Inc., 2010.

Hartzell, Bob. "How to Build an Electrician Career." eHow. com. Retrieved September 29, 2009 (http://www.ehow. com/how_5324594_build-electrician-career.html).

Overcamp, David. *Electrician* (High Interest Books). Danbury, CT: Children's Press, 2004.

bibliography

Black & Decker. *Advanced Home Wiring*. Minneapolis, MN: Creative Publishing International, 2009.

Black & Decker. *The Complete Guide to Wiring*. Minneapolis, MN: Creative Publishing International, 2008.

Brewer, Dennis C., and Paul A. Brewer. *Wiring Your Digital Home for Dummies*. Hoboken, NJ: Wiley Publishing, Inc., 2006.

Bureau of Labor Statistics. "Electricians." *Occupational Outlook Handbook, 2008–09*. U.S. Department of Labor. Retrieved September 22, 2009 (http://www.bls.gov/oco/ocos206.htm).

Career Key. "The Realistic Personality Type." Retrieved September 20, 2009 (http://www.careerkey.org/asp/your_personality/realistic_jump.htm).

CBC News. "Half of Ontarians Hire Unlicensed Electricians." September 24, 2009. Retrieved September 24, 2009 (http://www.cbc.ca/consumer/story/2009/09/24/contractors-electrical.html).

Construction Craft Training Center. "Journeyman Exam 1." Retrieved August 5, 2009 (http://www.cctc.edu/TEST_journeyman_exam_3.htm).

Farr, Michael. *300 Best Jobs for the 21st Century*. 4th ed. Indianapolis, IN: JIST Publishing, Inc., 2006.

Farr, Michael. *300 Best Jobs Without a Four-Year Degree*. 2nd ed. Indianapolis, IN: JIST Publishing, Inc., 2006.

Farr, Michael, and Laurence Shatkin. *225 Best Jobs for Baby Boomers*. Indianapolis, IN: JIST Publishing, Inc., 2007.

Fuller, Lucosi. "How to Become a Licensed Electrician in Canada." eHow.com. Retrieved September 21, 2009 (http://www.ehow.com/how_5036061_become-licensed-electrician-canada.html).

HowToDoThings.com. "How to Find Electrician Apprentice Jobs." Retrieved September 23, 2009 (http://www.howtodothings.com/careers/how-to-find-electrician-apprentice-jobs).

Johnsson, Julie. "McPier Sends 100 Electricians Away." *Chicago Tribune*, September 23, 2009. Retrieved September 23, 2009 (http://www.chicagotribune.com/business/chi-biz-mcpier-electricians-sep23,0,1837746.story).

Matthews, Marion. Personal Interview, September 2009.

Nemko, Marty. *Cool Careers for Dummies*. 3rd ed. Hoboken, NJ: Wiley Publishing, Inc., 2007.

O*NET Online. "Summary Report for: 47-2111.00 – Electricians." Retrieved September 19, 2009 (http://online.onetcenter.org/link/summary/47-2111.00).

Penn Foster Career School. "Electrician—Program Interview." Retrieved September 2009 (http://www.pennfoster.edu/electrician).

Politano, Anna. "Jobs with Power." *South Carolina Living*, September 2009, pp. 16–18.

Richter, H. P., et al. *Wiring Simplified*. 41st ed. Minneapolis, MN: Park Publishing, Inc., 2005.

Shatkin, Laurence. *Great Jobs in the President's Stimulus Plan*. Indianapolis, IN: JIST Publishing, 2009.

Shatkin, Laurence. *150 Best Recession-Proof Jobs*. Indianapolis, IN: JIST Publishing, 2009.

Strauss, Robert. "Repairman's Advantage: Even in Hard Times, Things Need to Be Fixed." *New York Times*, August 6, 2009. Retrieved August 11, 2009 (http://www.nytimes.com/2009/08/06/business/smallbusiness/06sbiz.html).

Van Liew, Jerry. Personal Interview, August 2009.

Wing, Charlie. *How Your House Works: A Visual Guide to Understanding & Maintaining Your Home*. Kingston, MA: Reed Construction Data, Inc., 2007.

index

ABOUT THE AUTHOR

Daniel E. Harmon is the author of more than seventy books and numerous magazine and newspaper articles. His previous career books for the Rosen Publishing Group include *Careers in the Corrections System*, *Careers in Explosives and Arson Investigation*, *First Job Smarts*, and *Jobs in Environmental Cleanup and Emergency Hazmat Response*. He lives in Spartanburg, South Carolina.

PHOTO CREDITS

Cover (background), p. 1 © www.istockphoto.com/DSGpro; cover (inset) Jose Luis Pelaez/Blend Images/Getty Images; p. 4 © www.istockphoto.com/David Lewis; p. 6 © www.istockphoto.com/zilli; pp. 9, 12–13, 20, 23, 33, 40–41, 48–49 Shutterstock.com; p. 11 © www.istockphoto.com/ Mike Cherim; pp. 16–17 © Florence Low/Sacramento Bee/ Zuma Press; pp. 26–27, 30, 44 © AP Images; p. 28 © www.istockphoto.com/photoBears; pp. 34–35 © John Gibbins/ The San Diego Union-Tribune/Zuma Press; pp. 38–39 © www.istockphoto.com/Bart Coenders; pp. 46–47 © Mack Goethe/St. Petersburg Times/Zuma Press; p. 58 © Dirk Shadd/St Petersburg Times/Zuma Press; p. 60 © Lannis Waters/The Palm Beach Post/Zuma Press; pp. 62–63 © Kin Man Hui/San Antonio Express-News/Zuma Press; p. 65 © Lezlie Sterling/Sacramento Bee/Zuma Press; p. 68 krtphotos/ Newscom.com.

Designer: Matthew Cauli; Editor: Kathy Kuhtz Campbell; Photo Researcher: Amy Feinberg